How to Draw
DOGS & PUPPIES

Learn to draw **20** dog breeds, step by easy step, shape by simple shape!

Illustrated by Diana Fisher

Walter Foster Jr.

Getting Started

When you look closely at the drawings in this book, you'll notice that they're made up of basic shapes, such as circles, triangles, and rectangles. To draw any dog or puppy, just start with simple shapes as you see here. It's easy and fun!

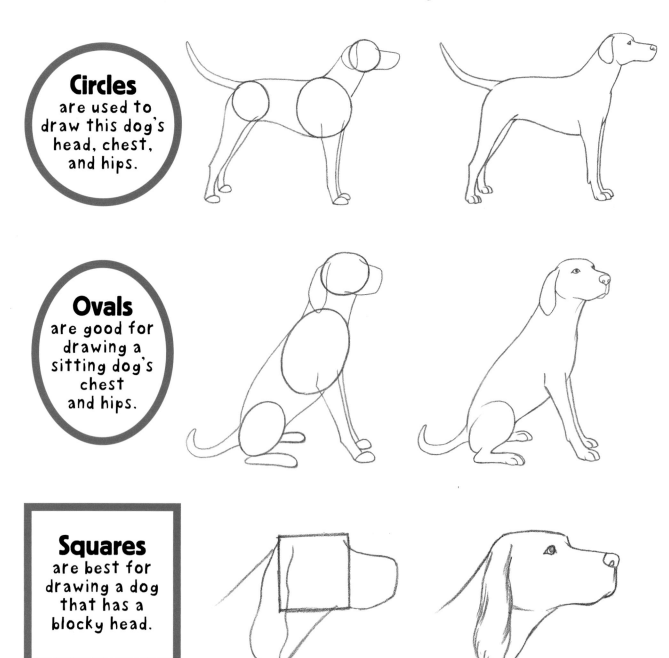

Circles are used to draw this dog's head, chest, and hips.

Ovals are good for drawing a sitting dog's chest and hips.

Squares are best for drawing a dog that has a blocky head.

Tips

There's more than one way to bring your furry friends to life on paper—you can use crayons, markers, or pencils. Just be sure you have black, brown, and white, plus yellow, orange, and red.

Pencils

Crayons

Markers

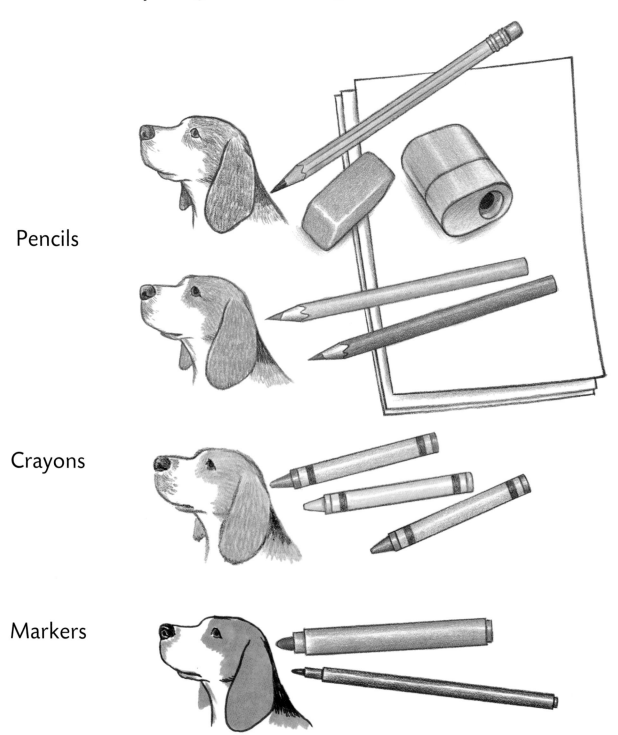

Pug Puppy

Adult Pugs have square faces with deep wrinkles. This Pug is just a pup, so its face is smoother and more rounded.

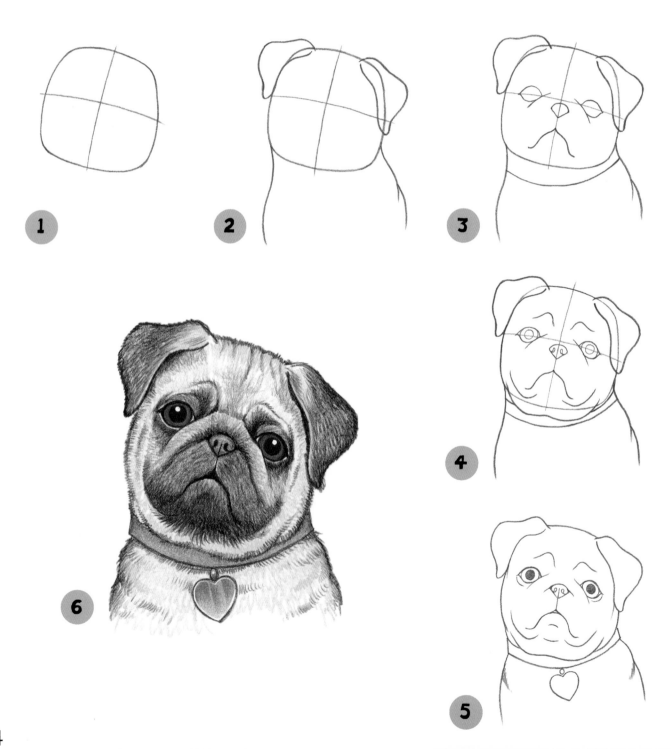

1

2

3

4

5

6

Chihuahua

Use circles for the chihuahua's tiny body. Then draw short legs. Be sure to add big, round eyes and large, triangular ears!

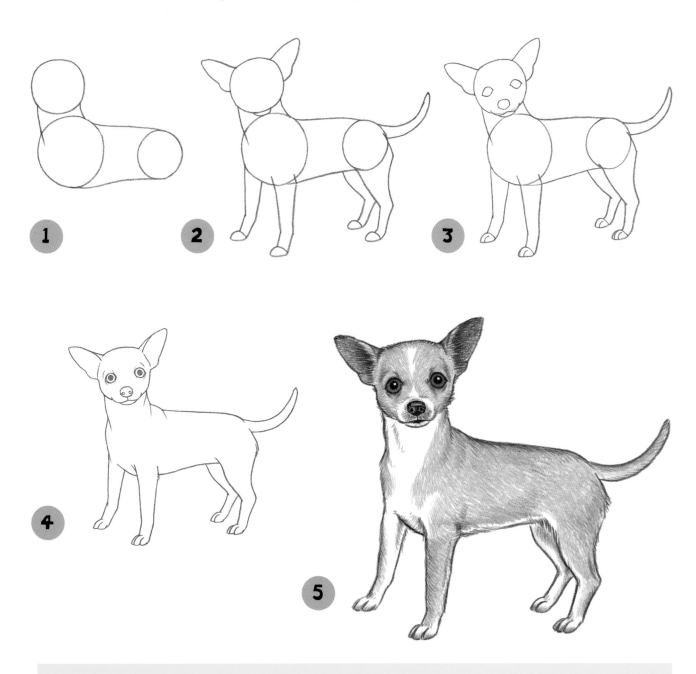

fun fact The Chihuahua is the smallest breed of dog! A full-grown Chihuahua measures from 6 to 9 inches (15.24 to 22.86 cm) tall at the shoulder and weighs only 2 to 6 pounds (0.9 to 2.7 kg)!

Great Dane

This gentle giant is very tall with a long body. Draw a big circle for the chest. Then add the head and hips with smaller circles.

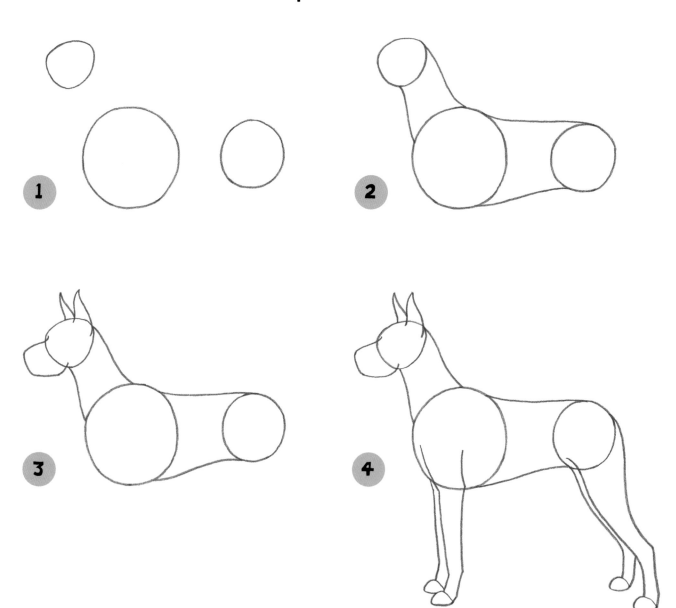

fun fact

The name "Great Dane" makes people think these dogs are Danish (from Denmark). But the Great Dane (also known as Deutsche Dogge, meaning "German Dog") is the national dog of Germany, where the breed originated.

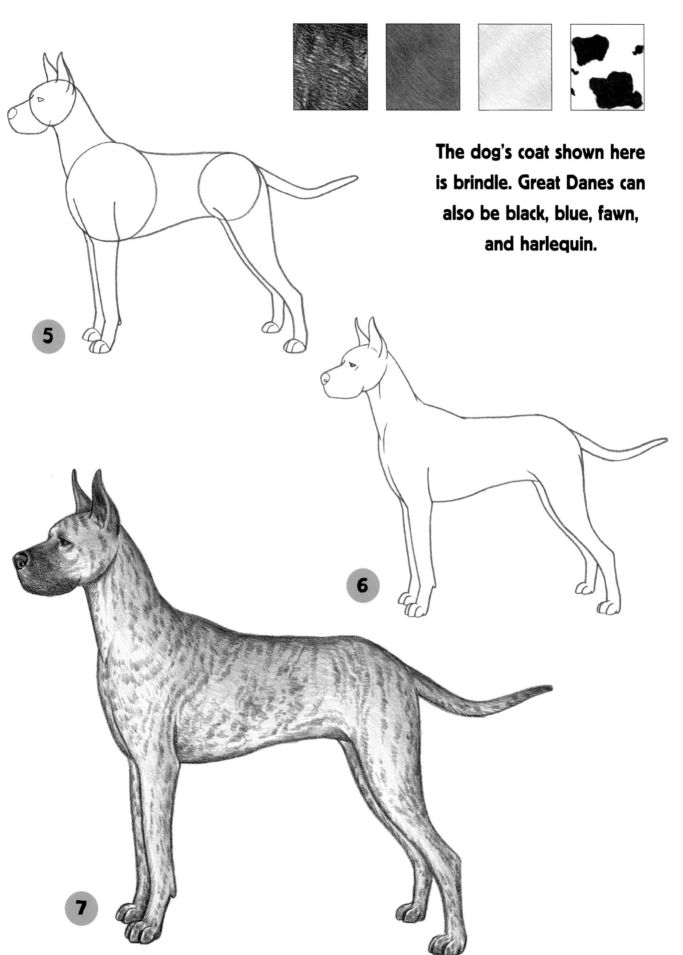

The dog's coat shown here is brindle. Great Danes can also be black, blue, fawn, and harlequin.

5

6

7

Beagle

When drawing this popular hound,
look at its unique features, such as its straight
forelegs, upright tail, and long ears.

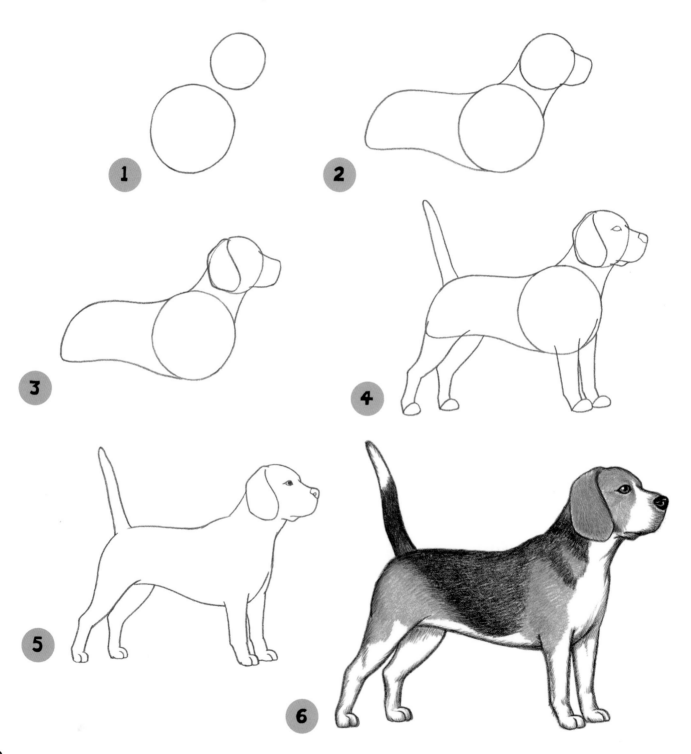

Scottish Terrier

Scottie dogs have many unusual features, including a long head, ears that stand up straight, a bushy beard, and "eyebrow" tufts.

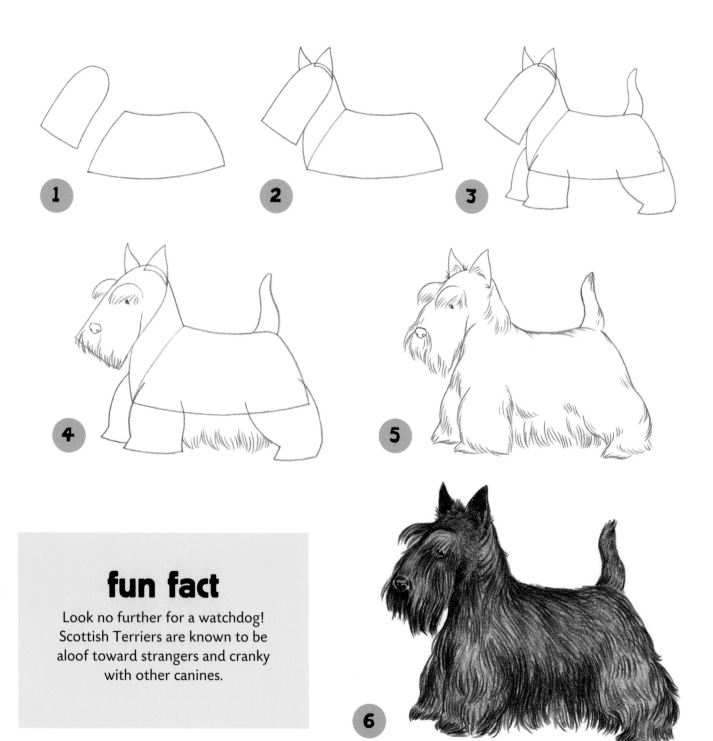

fun fact

Look no further for a watchdog! Scottish Terriers are known to be aloof toward strangers and cranky with other canines.

Airedale Terrier

This bearded breed has a flat, deep chest,
so start by drawing an oval for the body.
Then add a rectangle for the head.

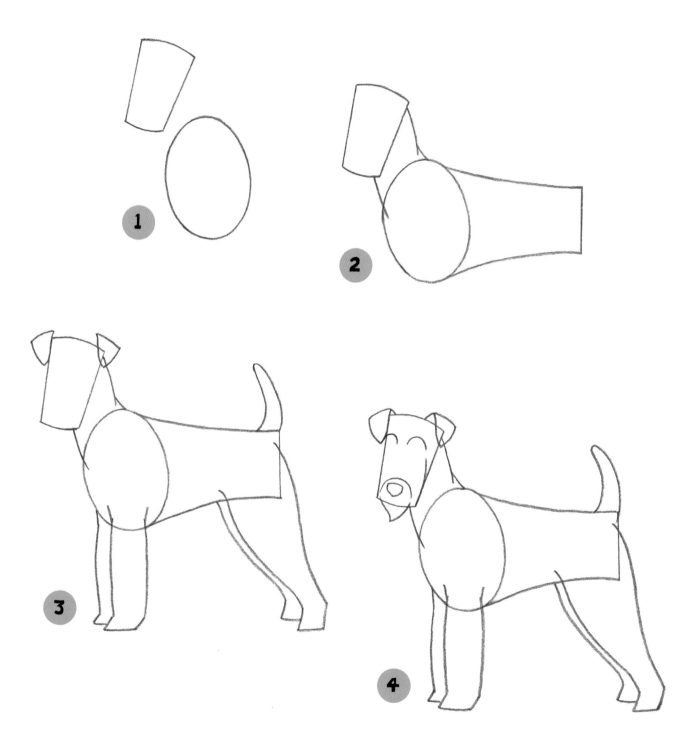

5

fun fact

The largest of all the terrier breeds, the Airedale is sometimes called "King of the Terriers." These noble dogs served in World War I, carrying messages and detecting approaching enemies. Their heroism made them popular during the 1920s.

6

Pomeranian

The Pom's body is very round, making this small pup look like a circular bundle of fur with tiny legs!

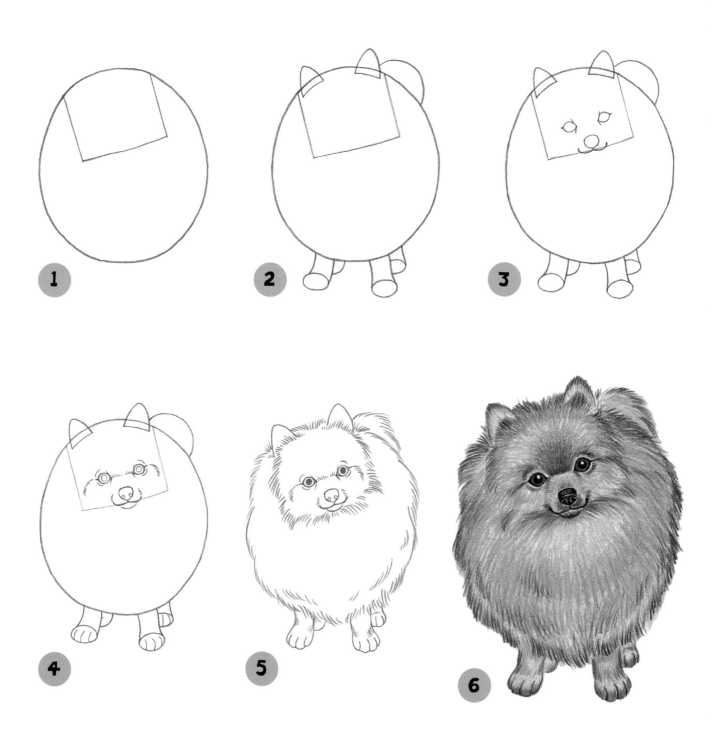

Parson Russell Terrier Puppy

These lovable pups are white with patches of black or tan. Their bright eyes are large and round, and their ears fold forward.

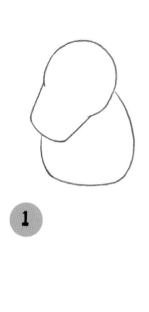

1

2

3

4

5

Golden Retriever Puppy

Best known for their shining coats, Goldens
also have strong legs, round paws,
and large, wide-set eyes.

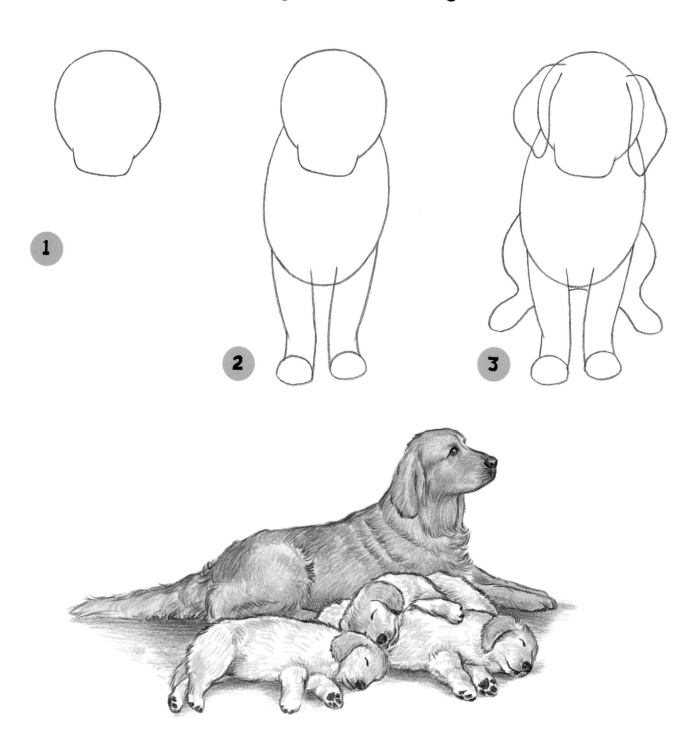

fun fact

Since the Golden Retriever was developed in England and Scotland in the 1800s, it has had many names. Until 1920, the breed was known as the Golden Flat-Coat. They've also been called "Yellow Retrievers" and "Russian Retrievers."

The rich, golden coat of this retriever comes in various shades—from light to dark.

Bouvier des Flandres

This shaggy herding dog has a rough coat, a thick beard, and a "fall" of hair that covers its eyes.

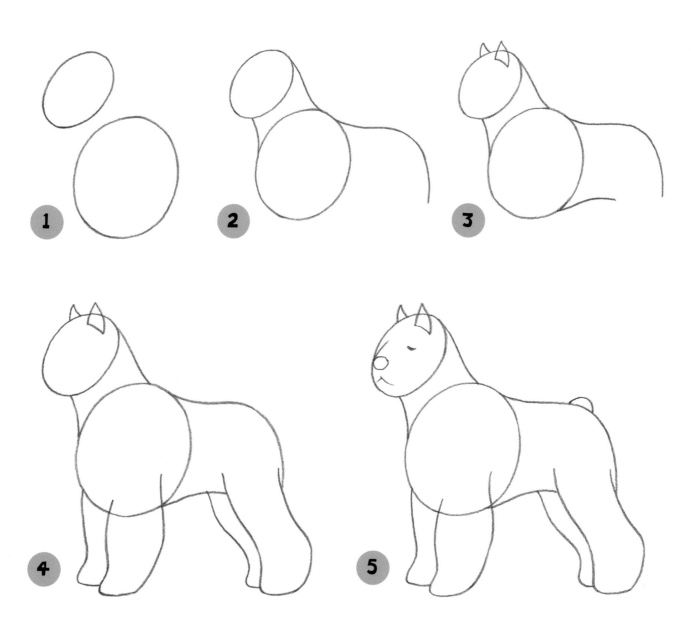

fun fact

The Bouvier's name reflects its birthplace. "Des Flandres" means "from Flanders," referring to the Northern region of Belgium where these loyal farm dogs originated.

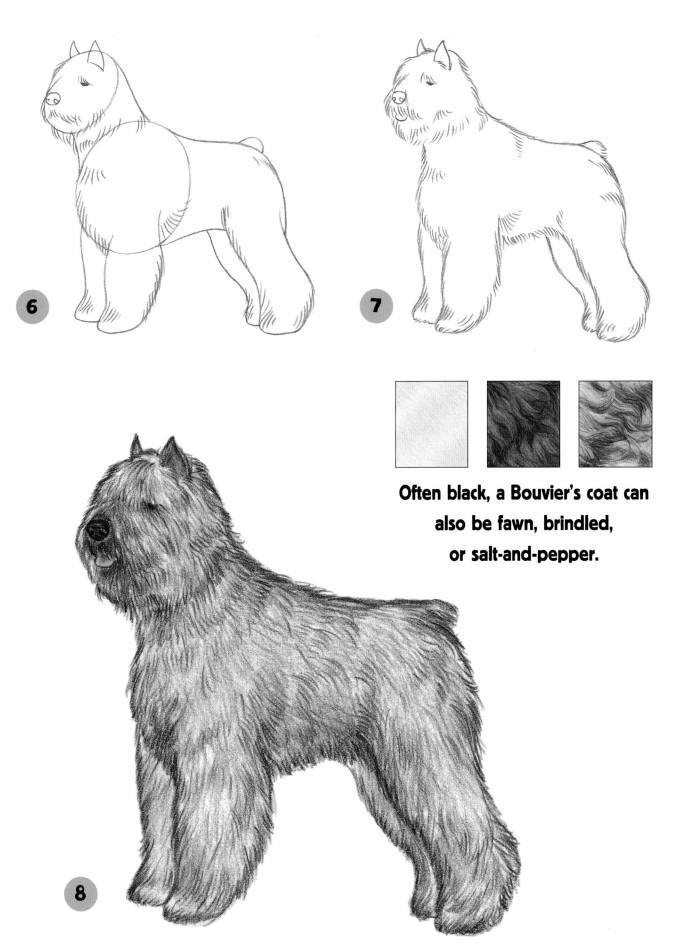

6

7

Often black, a Bouvier's coat can
also be fawn, brindled,
or salt-and-pepper.

8

English Springer Spaniel

The lively Springer is a hunting dog with long ears, a round head, and a rectangular muzzle.

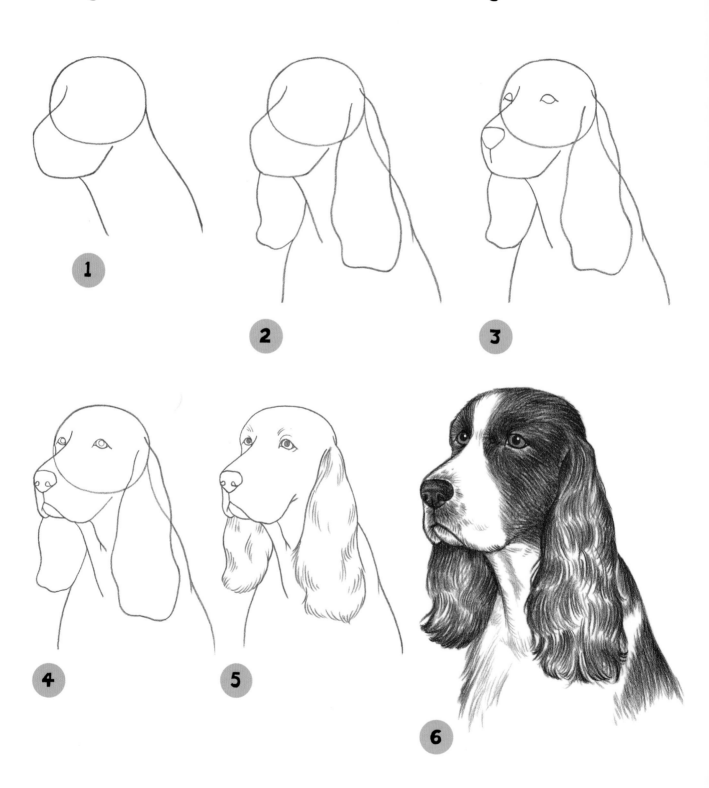

Dachshund

These low-to-the-ground pooches have long, thin bodies with a sausage shape.

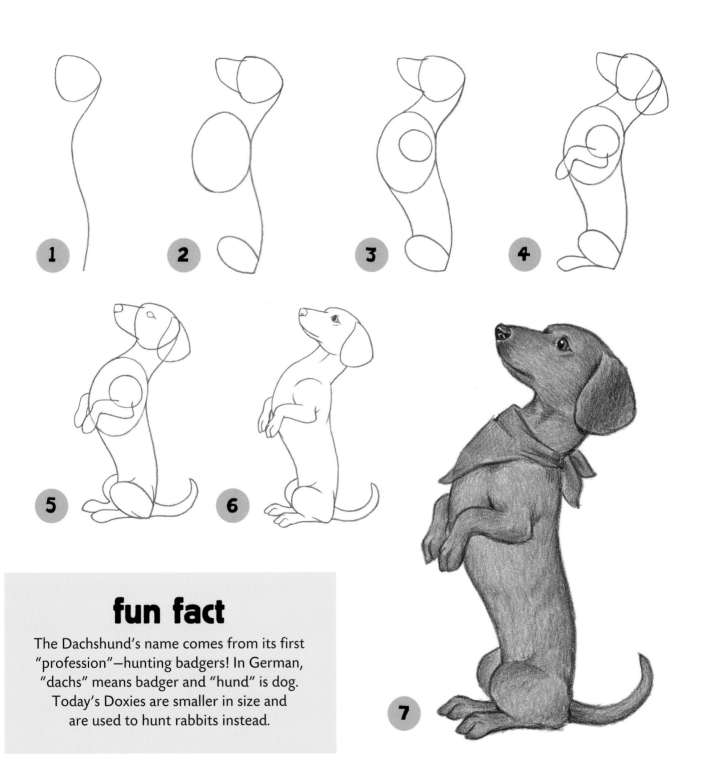

fun fact

The Dachshund's name comes from its first "profession"—hunting badgers! In German, "dachs" means badger and "hund" is dog. Today's Doxies are smaller in size and are used to hunt rabbits instead.

Dalmatian Puppy

It's easy to spot a Dalmatian! Dals have round markings, round hips, and rounded ears.

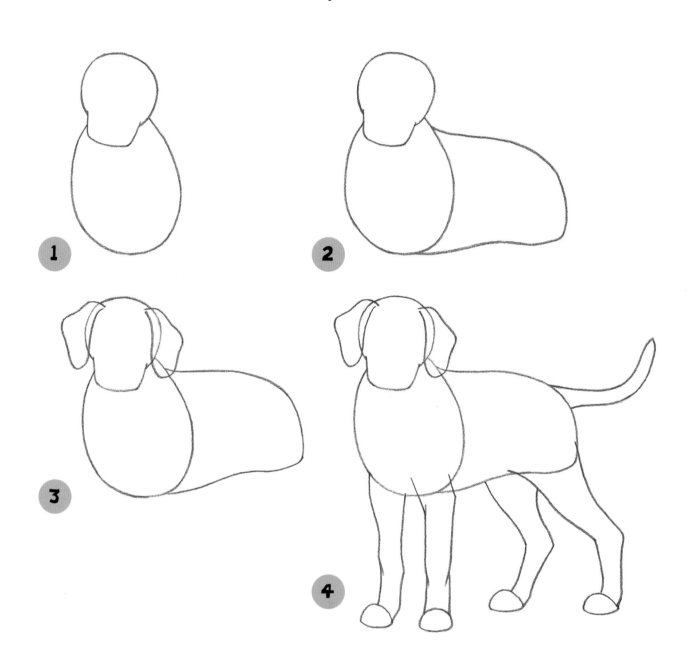

fun fact

Dalmatian puppies are born with solid white coats! When they are between 2 and 6 weeks old, they begin to develop spots. The spots continue to grow until the pups are about 6 months old.

5

6

7

Siberian Husky

The Husky is a sled dog with an athletic body. Draw an oval to create this dog's deep chest— and don't forget its bushy tail!

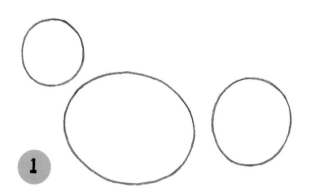

fun fact

Siberian Huskies are known for their striking eyes, which range from sky blue to reddish amber.
It is not uncommon for a Husky to have two eyes of different hues (called "bi-eyed") or for a Husky to have one eye of two different hues (called "parti-eyed").

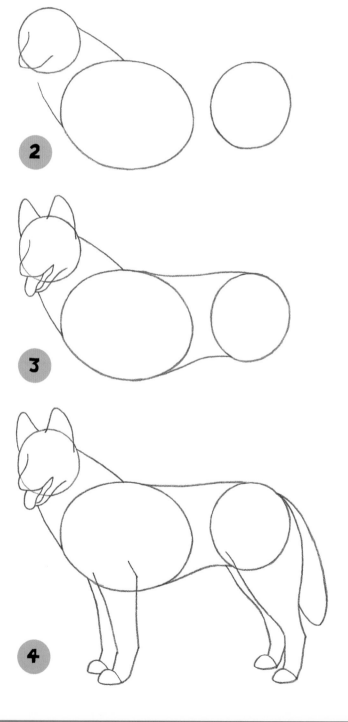

In addition to the black and white shown here, a Husky's coat can be salt and pepper, red and white, or solid white.

5

6

7

Papillon

In French, *papillon* means "butterfly."
These dogs were named for their large,
fringed ears that resemble butterfly wings!

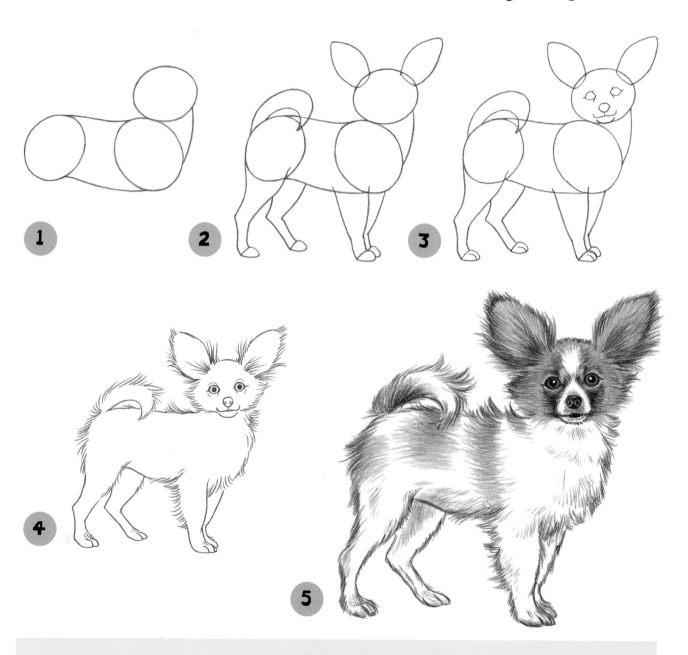

fun fact

In the 1600s, Papillons were known as Dwarf Spaniels, and they had "drop ears" that hung down. The breed was renamed when puppies began appearing with large, pricked ears. Today's Papillons may have either ear type.

Puli

With their long cords of hair that look like dreadlocks, Pulik (the plural of Puli) mop up attention! The cords are shorter on their heads.

1

2

3

4

5

6

German Shepherd

This popular breed has a long, strong body.
Be sure to draw large, athletic thighs on
this proud, powerful canine—and make its muzzle
about half the length of its head.

fun fact

German Shepherds are often used as guard dogs, police dogs, and military dogs. Intelligent and hard working, these canines also help detect drugs and bombs, perform search-and-rescue missions, and track missing persons.

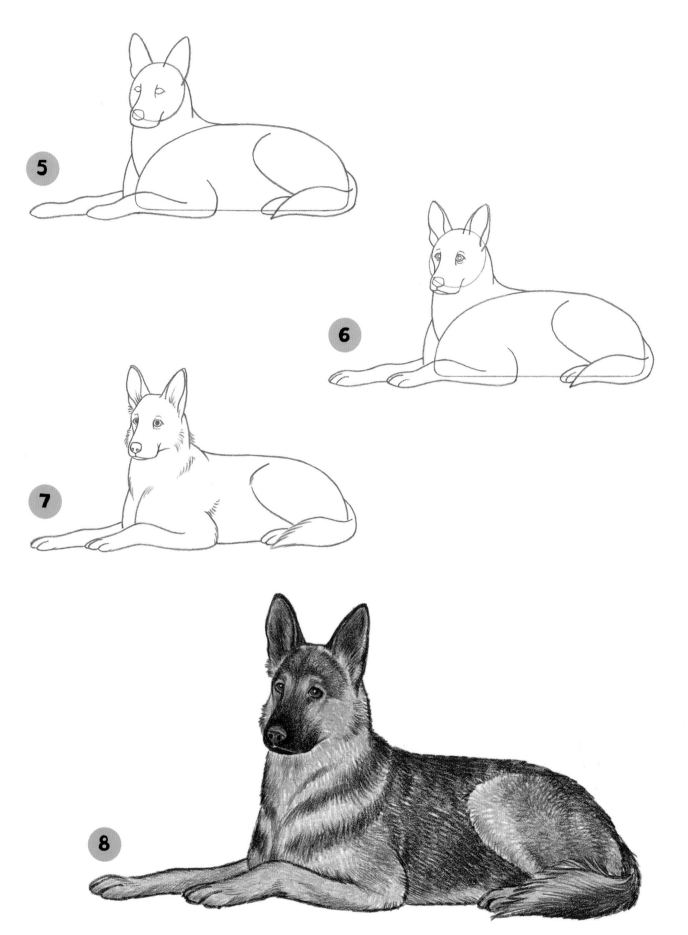

5

6

7

8

Standard Poodle

The traditional Poodle cut—which includes pompoms—shows off the Standard Poodle's pointed muzzle and muscular hind legs.

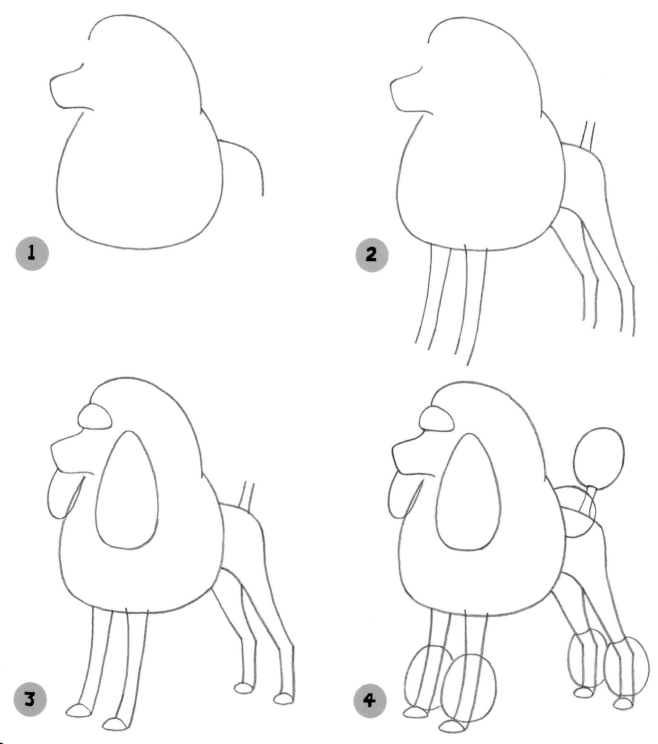

fun fact

Many people call the Standard Poodle a "French Poodle" because of its history as a show dog and circus dog in France. But this breed actually originated in Germany. Bred as a duck retriever, the Poodle's name comes from the German word *pudelin*, which means "to splash in water." The Standard Poodle's traditional haircut makes it easier for the dog to swim; the pompoms of fur keep the dog's joints warm.

Rough Collie

The Rough collie's mane is eye-catching because it is so full and bushy—much like the breed's long, fluffy tail. But the feature the collie is best known for is its intelligent expression!

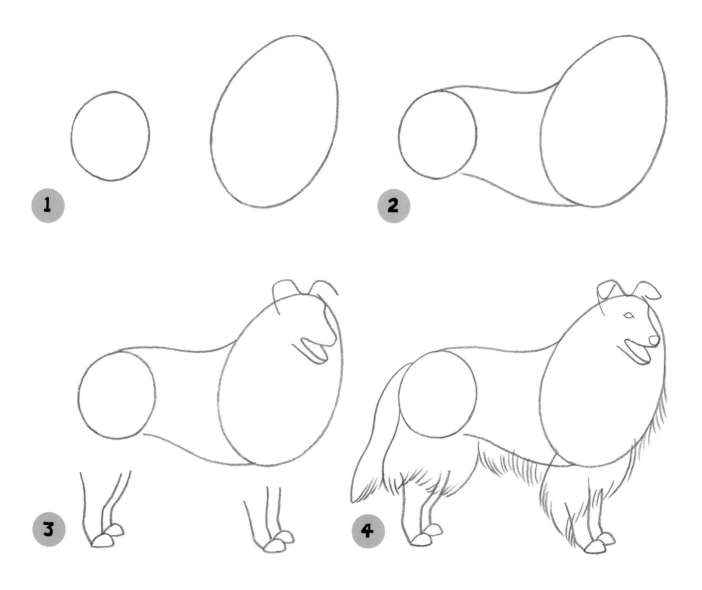

fun fact

Originally a sheep-herding dog in Scotland, the Rough Collie developed a thick, fluffy coat to keep it warm during the cold and harsh weather.

5

6

7

The Collie shown here
is sable and white.
They can also be white,
tricolor, or blue merle.

Australian Shepherd Puppies

The thick ruff of fur on an Australian Shepherd's neck and chest combines with round, wide-set eyes and triangular, high-set ears to give this herding dog a playful look!